THE GROSS HUMAN BODY IN ACTION
AUGMENTED REALITY

A Revolting AUGMENTED REALITY Experience

Percy Leed

Lerner Publications ◆ Minneapolis

EXPLORE THE HUMAN BODY IN BRAND-NEW WAYS WITH AUGMENTED REALITY!

1. Ask a parent or guardian for permission to download the free Lerner AR app on your digital device by going to the App Store or Google Play. When you launch the app, choose the Gross Human Body series.

2. As you read, look for this icon throughout the book. It means there is an augmented reality experience on that page!

3. Use the Lerner AR app to scan the picture near the icon.

4. Watch the human body's systems come alive with augmented reality!

CONTENTS

INTRODUCTION
BLOODY HEALING

Have you ever crashed your bike and cut your knee? Or have you been hit in the face by a ball and gotten a big shiny bruise? Have any of your scabs oozed with disgusting pus?

A black eye is a bruise caused by blood pooling under your skin.

A scrape stings, but it heals quickly if you keep it clean and cover it with a bandage.

Not only do wounds hurt, but they look nasty too. But don't worry. When you fall off your bike and your knee looks like bloody hamburger meat, your body gets busy repairing the damage. Blood, bruises, and scabs are all part of healing.

SCRAPES AND SCABS: SHREDDING SKIN

When you rip a hole in your skin, your blood gets to work. It rushes special cells, called platelets, to the injury. Platelets are like your body's glue. They make a clot, a sticky glob that stops the bleeding. If your blood does not clot, you could bleed to death.

By the time you look down to see the damage, your body has already begun to stop the bleeding.

This image of platelets (*colored blue*) and red blood cells was created with a special microscope.

As platelets plug the injury, they also send a shout-out to clotting proteins in the body. When these chemicals receive the signal, they rush to the wound. Clotting proteins get right to work helping platelets make a web. The web helps hold the clot in place. It also catches blood cells.

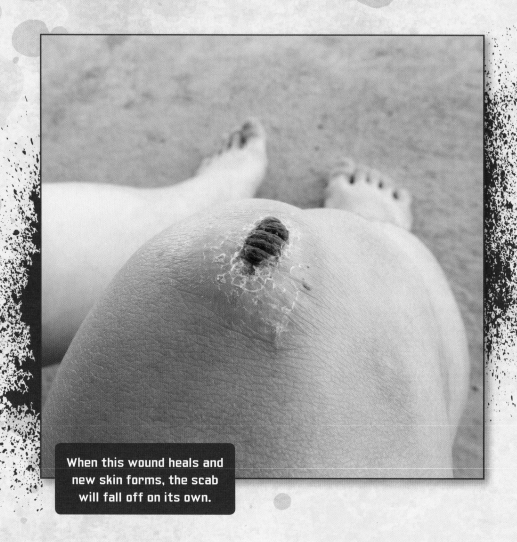

When this wound heals and new skin forms, the scab will fall off on its own.

The web dries and hardens to form a scab. The blood cells caught in the web give the scab a reddish-brown color. Yep, scabs are just bloody plugs. But don't get too grossed out. Scabs are protecting new skin that's forming under them.

By the time a big bloody scab stops the flow of blood, healing is well underway. Your body is already forming new skin. Sometimes when the scab falls off, the new skin looks different from the skin around it. That's because it's a scar.

Most scars are flat and pale. Bor-ing! But keloid scars are raised or bumpy. Other scars look like pits or craters. These sunken scars are often caused by acne, chicken pox, or surgery cuts. Whatever kind of scars you end up with, you can enjoy them for a long time. Even if they fade over time, they'll probably never totally go away.

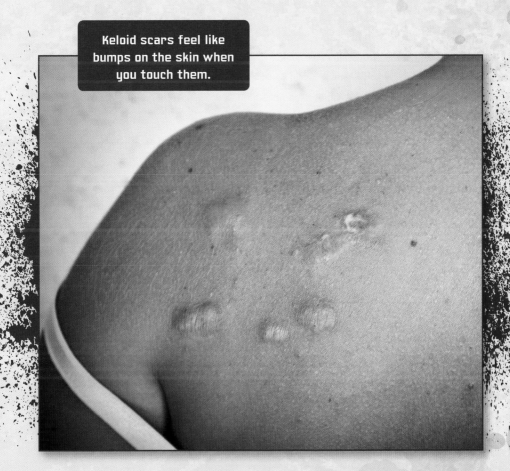

Keloid scars feel like bumps on the skin when you touch them.

Scars are a normal part of healing, but some people don't like the way scars look. To keep a wound from becoming a big scar, you may have to get stitches. Stitches are used for really bad cuts. To stitch you up, a doctor uses a needle and thread just as people use when they make clothes. Ow!

Some stitches must be removed after the wound heals. Others break down and disappear on their own.

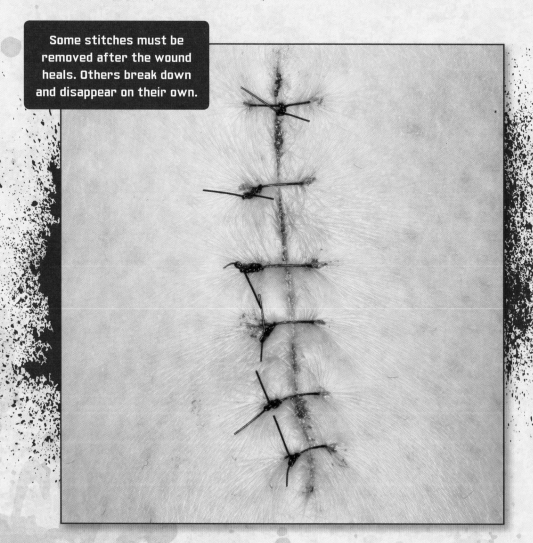

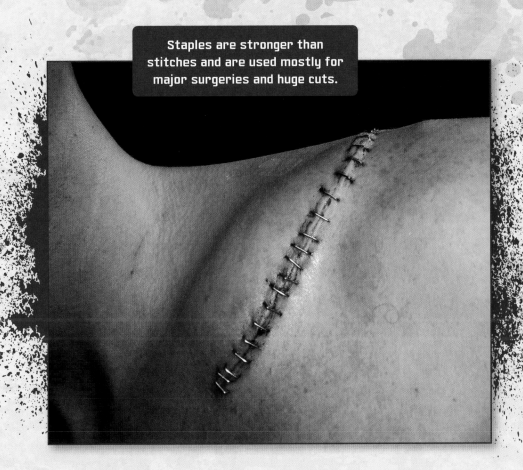

Staples are stronger than stitches and are used mostly for major surgeries and huge cuts.

Instead of stitches, a doctor might staple your wound shut. Surgical staples look a lot like regular staples. Stapling a wound is a lot faster than stitching it. Now hold still . . . *KA-CHUNK!*

CHAPTER 2

FULL OF LIFE: BLOOD'S EVERYBODY'S BUDDY

Bike riding can get bloody. After all, you're not really having fun until you leave a chunk of yourself on the street, right? When you crash and bleed, where does all that red stuff come from?

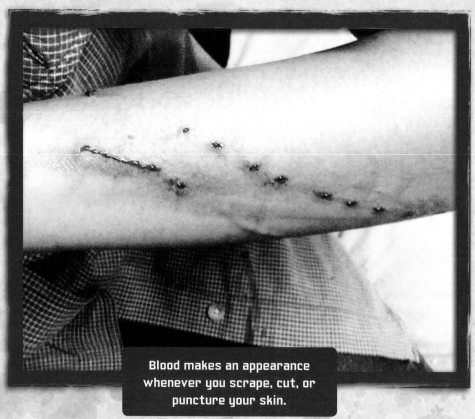

Blood makes an appearance whenever you scrape, cut, or puncture your skin.

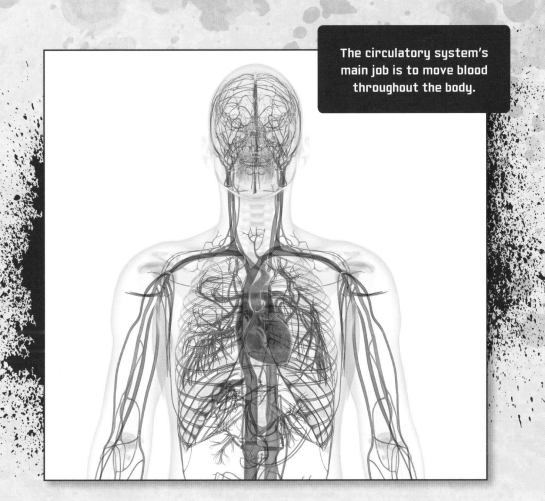

Blood carries nutrients and oxygen to the body's cells. It also carries carbon dioxide, a chemical your cells don't need. They ship it off in the blood to the lungs. And then, bye-bye! Your lungs get rid of the carbon dioxide by breathing it out.

Blood moves in tubes called blood vessels. The heart is a powerful muscle that squeezes and pumps blood throughout the body. The heart and blood vessels make up the body's circulatory system.

You have three types of blood vessels: arteries, veins, and capillaries. Arteries carry blood away from the heart to other parts of the body. Veins carry the blood back to the heart.

Capillaries are tiny blood vessels that connect arteries and veins. While blood moves through capillaries, oxygen seeps

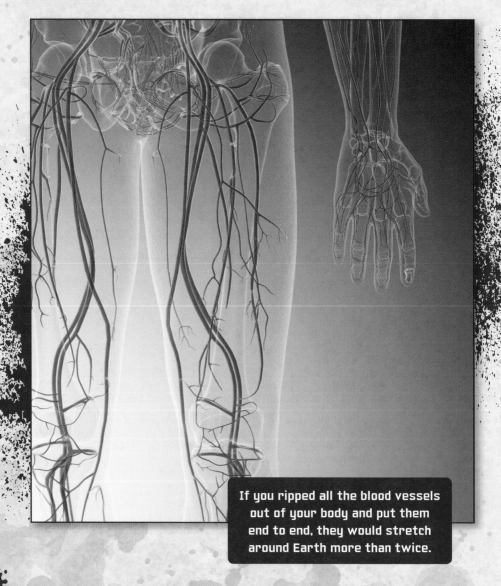

If you ripped all the blood vessels out of your body and put them end to end, they would stretch around Earth more than twice.

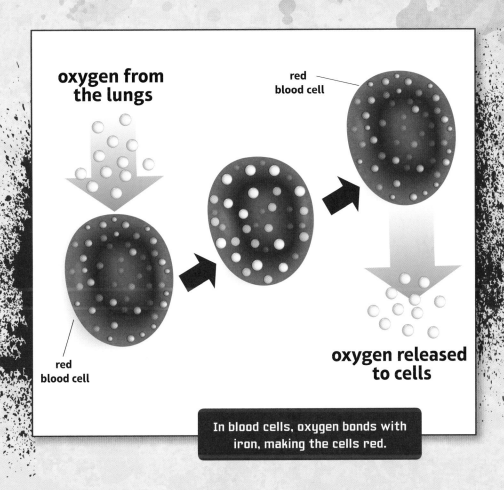

**oxygen from
the lungs**

red
blood cell

red
blood cell

**oxygen released
to cells**

In blood cells, oxygen bonds with
iron, making the cells red.

out of them and into the body's cells where it's needed. In
return, the cells send carbon dioxide into the capillaries.

After blood has traded its oxygen for carbon dioxide,
capillaries send the blood into the veins. The heart pumps it
to the lungs. Then you breathe out the carbon dioxide and
breathe in more oxygen, and the cycle starts again. Your
body circulates blood day and night and never takes a break.
This is the stuff vampires dream about.

Blood contains platelets, red blood cells, and white blood cells. Remember platelets? Those blood cells that help you not bleed to death? Red blood cells contain the protein hemoglobin. It carries oxygen to the body's cells and takes carbon dioxide away.

Red blood cells in a blood vessel

Oxygen-rich red blood cells
flow through an artery.

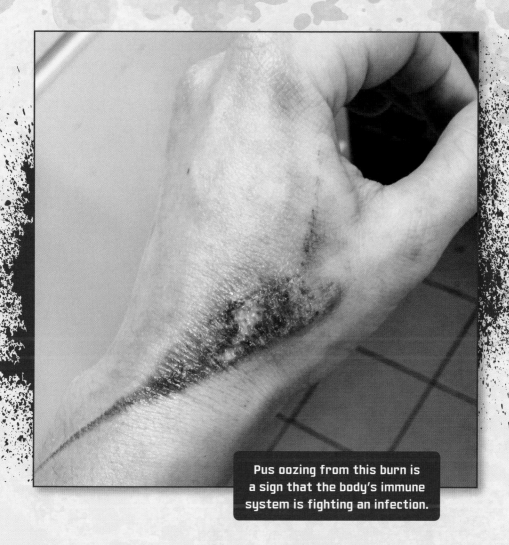

Pus oozing from this burn is a sign that the body's immune system is fighting an infection.

Sometimes germs get into your body through a wound and cause an infection that makes you sick. As soon as your immune system senses an invasion, it calls on the body's soldiers—white blood cells. Their job is to kill germs.

If a cut gets infected, it sometimes swells up and oozes pus. Pus is sticky, clumpy gunk, but it's a good sign. It means your immune system is working. Pus is made up of white blood cells that died in the battle against your infection.

CHAPTER 3

FLOW, GUSH, AND POOL: ALL ABOUT BLEEDING

If you get a really bad cut, your body can have trouble stopping the bleeding. So be careful when playing with swords and battle-axes. A deep cut can quickly become dangerous if the bleeding isn't stopped. Pressure to the wound usually works, but if bleeding continues for fifteen

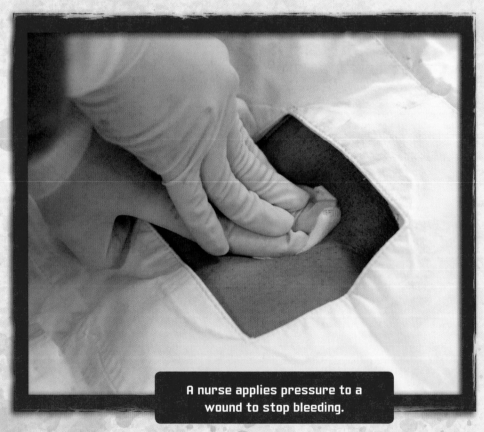

A nurse applies pressure to a wound to stop bleeding.

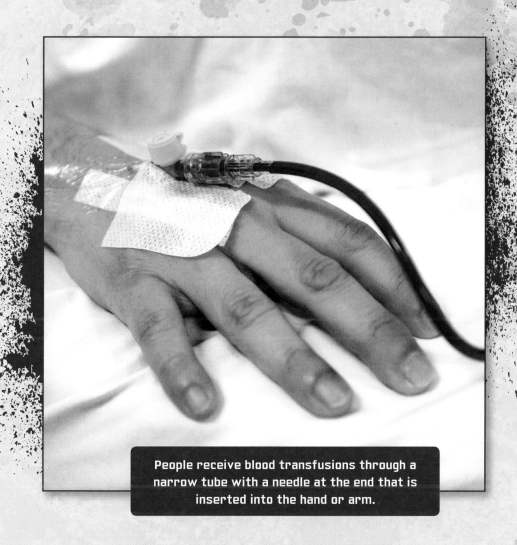

People receive blood transfusions through a narrow tube with a needle at the end that is inserted into the hand or arm.

minutes, you need a doctor. Then you can explain to the doctor what you were doing with a battle-axe.

People who lose too much blood might feel dizzy. If bleeding continues, the person could die. To prevent that, a doctor might replace the lost blood with a transfusion—blood from another person put into the body. The blood could come from a relative or a stranger.

Blood comes in four types: A, B, AB, and O. Each one has slightly different proteins and other ingredients. People who need a transfusion must receive the right blood. If they receive the wrong type, they could die.

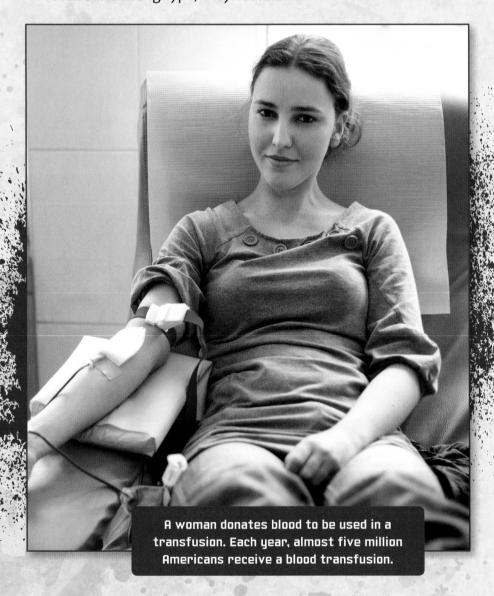

A woman donates blood to be used in a transfusion. Each year, almost five million Americans receive a blood transfusion.

Leech saliva has a chemical that numbs
the spots leeches sink their teeth,
so you can't feel them bite.

Doctors in ancient times made people bleed on purpose.
They believed bleeding could cure almost anything.
Sniffles? You might need a good bleeding. Headache? Bleed
it out.

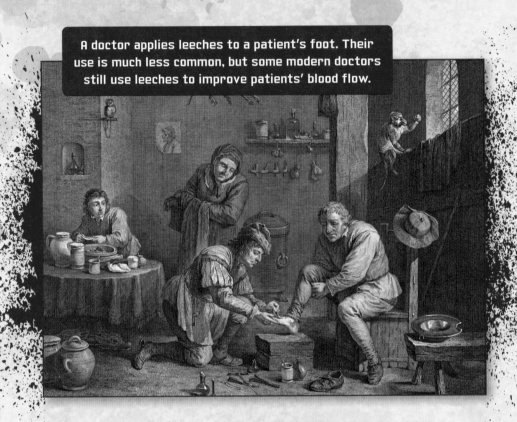

A doctor applies leeches to a patient's foot. Their use is much less common, but some modern doctors still use leeches to improve patients' blood flow.

One way doctors got the blood flowing was with leeches. Leeches are bloodsucking worms that doctors used in places their knives couldn't reach, such as gums, lips, or inside the nose. Yikes!

Leeches have a chemical in their spit that prevents clotting, so they can slurp from the blood buffet as long as they like. Vampire bats, mosquitoes, fleas, and ticks all chow down on blood. Like leeches, most of these animals have chemicals that numb their victims and prevent clotting.

Some bleeding occurs inside the body. When you get smacked in the arm, capillaries can be damaged. Blood leaks from them and pools under your skin as a bruise.

Bruises change color over time as the blood breaks down. They go from reddish to purplish black to a puke-green color. They appear light brown after a couple of weeks and then disappear as your body reabsorbs all the blood.

Bruise

This bruise is changing from purplish black to puke green.

CHAPTER 4

STOP, CLOT, AND ROT: THE FLOW STOPS HERE

Scabs are blood clots on the outside of our bodies. However, blood clots also form inside blood vessels. Some of these clots can be very dangerous.

If a clot prevents blood from flowing through blood vessels properly, cells and organs can't get the oxygen they need.

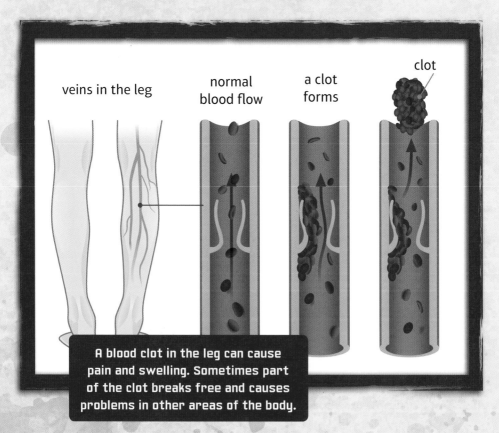

veins in the leg

normal blood flow

a clot forms

clot

A blood clot in the leg can cause pain and swelling. Sometimes part of the clot breaks free and causes problems in other areas of the body.

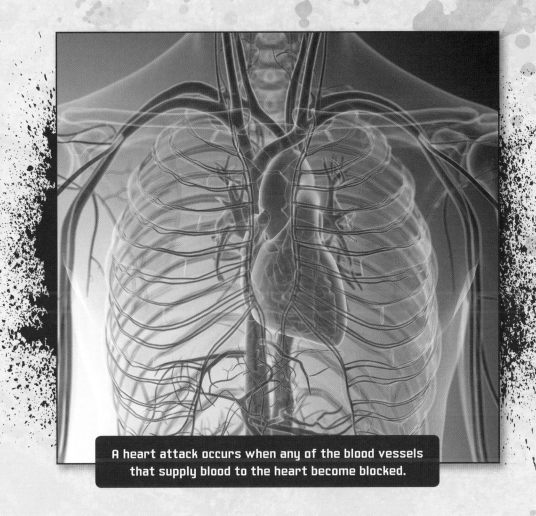

A heart attack occurs when any of the blood vessels
that supply blood to the heart become blocked.

A blood clot in the brain, for example, could damage the part
of the brain that can't get oxygen. A clot in the heart can
cause a heart attack. If the brain or heart are deprived of
oxygen long enough, death can result.

All organs and body parts need blood to bring them
oxygen. If hands or feet go too long without enough oxygen,
they die and begin to decay.

This decay, or gangrene, comes in two forms—dry or wet. Both are nasty. With dry gangrene, the skin and tissue of the affected area slowly dies. It becomes cold, black, and dry. After several weeks, the skin and tissue fall off.

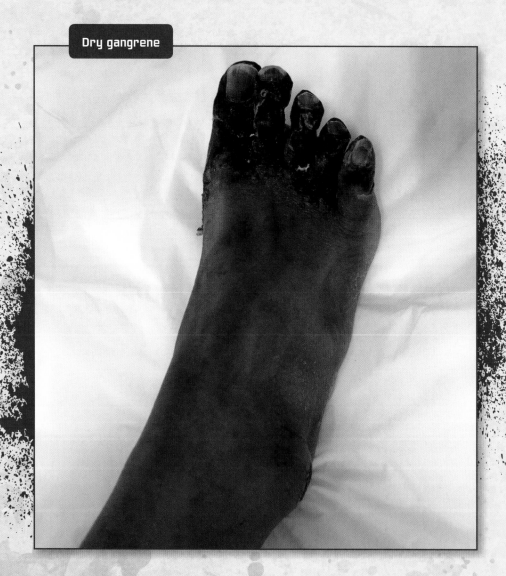

Dry gangrene

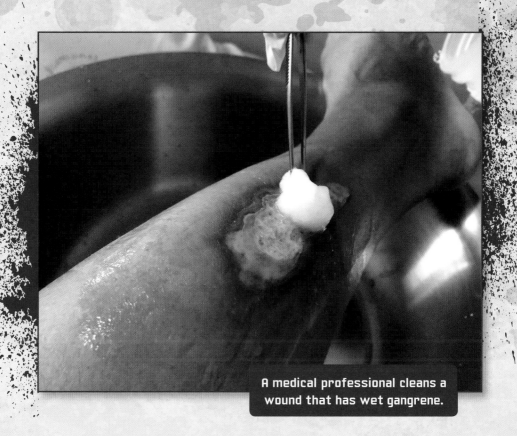

A medical professional cleans a wound that has wet gangrene.

When bacteria invade the tissue with gangrene, you're in even more trouble. If the bacteria cause an infection, you have wet gangrene. Lucky you! With little or no blood flow, white blood cells can't kill the bacteria. The bacteria grows and the tissue rots, turning black and smelly. Sometimes doctors have to cut off tissue with wet gangrene to stop the infection from spreading.

Most of the time, you don't have to worry about gangrene. Your blood will take care of everything for you. So relax the next time you make hamburger meat out of your arm while riding your bike. Your blood can handle it. Oh, except for the pain. You're on your own with that!

GROSS BLOOD FACTS

- Platelets and other blood cells are made in bone marrow, the squishy tissue that fills the inside of bones.

- Platelets age fast. If a platelet is not used to plug a cut within ten days of when the platelet is made, it dies.

- Picture five 1-liter bottles of soda pop lined up in a row. That's how much blood the average adult has running through the body.

- Every ten seconds, someone in the United States gets a blood transfusion.

- The study of blood is called hematology. Many other words that start with hema- or hemo- are blood related too. A hematoma, for example, is a bruise.

- Not all animals have red blood. Horseshoe crabs have blue blood. The blood of cockroaches is colorless. Some marine worms have green blood.

GLOSSARY

artery: a blood vessel that carries blood away from the heart

bacteria: tiny living things that live all around and inside you

capillary: a tiny blood vessel that connects arteries and veins

carbon dioxide: a gas without color or odor that the body breathes out as waste

immune system: the body's defense system against infection and disease

infection: the entry and growth of bacteria or other germs inside the body that makes a person sick

nutrient: a substance that helps growth, provides energy, and maintains life

platelet: a small blood cell necessary for blood clotting

protein: a chemical that is essential for life

pus: thick liquid containing dead white blood cells that comes from an infected wound

vein: a blood vessel that carries blood back to the heart from other parts of the body

FURTHER INFORMATION

Farndon, John. *Stickmen's Guide to Your Beating Heart*. Minneapolis: Hungry Tomato, 2017.

Farndon, John. *Tiny Killers: When Bacteria and Viruses Attack*. Minneapolis: Hungry Tomato, 2017.

Heart and Circulatory System
https://www.hopkinsallchildrens.org/Patients-Families
/Health-Library/HealthDocNew/Heart-and-Circulatory-System

Pettiford, Rebecca. *The Circulatory System*. Minneapolis: Bellwether Media, 2020.

Stiefel, Chana. *Animal Zombies! And Other Bloodsucking Beasts, Creepy Creatures, and Real-Life Monsters*. Washington, DC: National Geographic, 2018.

Vampire Bat
https://kids.nationalgeographic.com/animals/mammals
/vampire-bat/

Your Heart & Circulatory System
https://kidshealth.org/en/kids/heart.html

Your Immune System
https://kidshealth.org/en/kids/immune.html

INDEX

PHOTO ACKNOWLEDGMENTS

Image credits: Creatas Images/Getty Images, p. 4; kali9/Getty Images, p. 5; IRINA KROLEVETC/iStock/Getty Images, p. 6; STEVE GSCHMEISSNER/SCIENCE PHOTO LIBRARY/Getty Images, p. 7; PUGUN SJ/iStock/Getty Images, p. 8; piccerella/iStock/Getty Images, p. 9; spxChrome/Getty Images, p. 10; belterz/Getty Images, p. 11; Rosmah Abdul Hamid/EyeEm/Getty Images, p. 12; SCIEPRO/SCIENCE PHOTO LIBRARY/Getty Images, pp. 13, 14, 25; ttsz/iStock/Getty Images, p. 15; Christoph Burgstedt/Science Photo Library/Getty Images, p. 16; evgeny_pylayev/iStock/Getty Images, p. 17; PIJITRA PHOMKHAM/Shutterstock.com, p. 18; LordRunar/iStock/Getty Images, p. 19; JanekWD/Getty Images, p. 20; sydeen/Getty Images, p. 21; Keith Lance/Getty Images, p. 22; Ascent/PKS Media Inc./Getty Images, p. 23; solar22/iStock/Getty Images, p. 24; Duangnapa Kanchanasakun/Shutterstock.com, pp. 26, 27; AR Experience: TurboSquid, Inc. (leech 3D models). Design elements: EduardHarkonen/Getty Images; atakan/Getty Images; kaylabutler/Getty Images; Eratel/Getty Images; gadost/Getty Images; Freer/Shutterstock.com; Anastasiia_M/Getty Images (green slime frame); Anastasiia_M/Getty Images (green slime blot); amtitus/Getty Images; desifoto/Getty Images; Yevhenii Dubinko/Getty Images; arthobbit/Getty Images; cajoer/Getty Images; enjoynz/Getty Images.

Cover images: Dimarik/iStock/Getty Images; Mohammed Haneefa Nizamudeen/iStock/Getty Images.

Lerner Publications Company
An imprint of Lerner Publishing Group, Inc.
241 First Avenue North
Minneapolis, MN 55401 USA

For reading levels and more information, look up this title at www.lernerbooks.com.

Main body text set in Aptifer Sans LT Pro.
Typeface provided by Linotype AG.

Designer: Kimberly Morales
Lerner team: Martha Kranes

Library of Congress Cataloging-in-Publication Data

Names: Leed, Percy, 1968– author.
Title: Blood : a revolting augmented reality experience / Percy Leed.
Description: Minneapolis : Lerner Publications, [2021] | Series: The gross human body in action : augmented reality | Includes bibliographical references and index. | Audience: Ages 8–11 | Audience: Grades K–1 | Summary: "From bruises to clots, scabs, and arteries, learn all about the human circulatory system in disgusting detail." — Provided by publisher.
Identifiers: LCCN 2019045727 (print) | LCCN 2019045728 (ebook) | ISBN 9781541598089 (library binding) | ISBN 9781728401294 (ebook)
Subjects: LCSH: Cardiovascular system—Juvenile literature. | Blood—Juvenile literature.
Classification: LCC QM178 .H88 2021 (print) | LCC QM178 (ebook) | DDC 612.1/1—dc23

LC record available at https://lccn.loc.gov/2019045727
LC ebook record available at https://lccn.loc.gov/2019045728

Manufactured in the United States of America
1-47999-48677-1/15/2020